HAMMOND

the
explorer atlas

Mapmakers for the 21st Century

CONTENTS

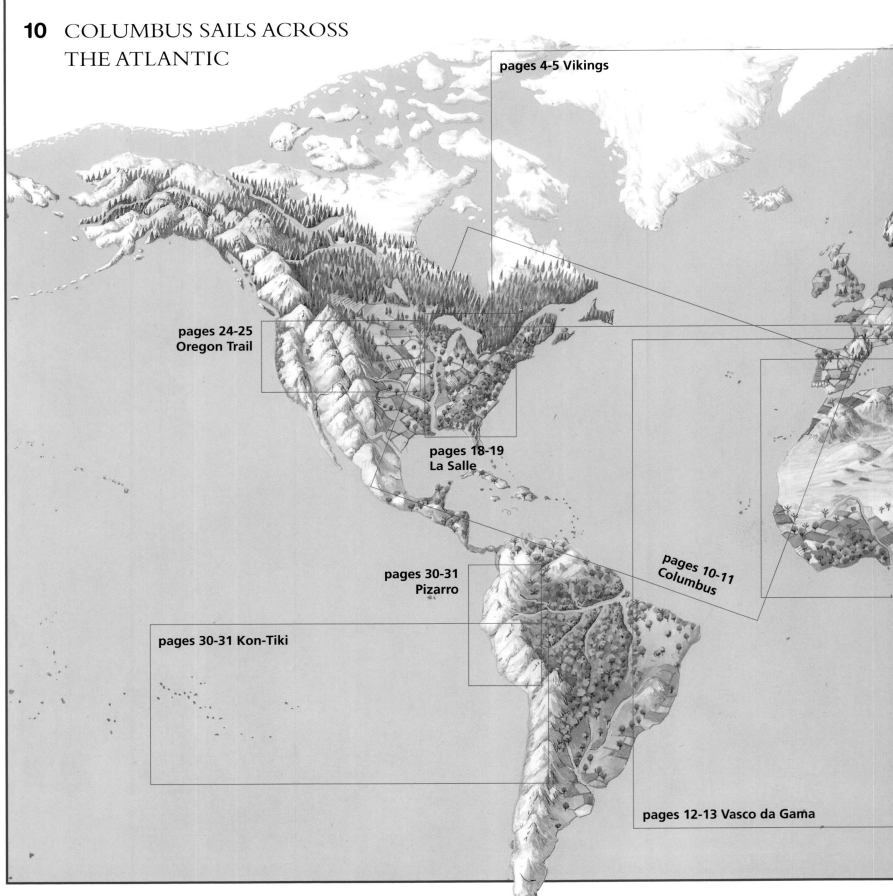

pages 4-5 Vikings

pages 24-25 Oregon Trail

pages 18-19 La Salle

pages 30-31 Pizarro

pages 10-11 Columbus

pages 30-31 Kon-Tiki

pages 12-13 Vasco da Gama

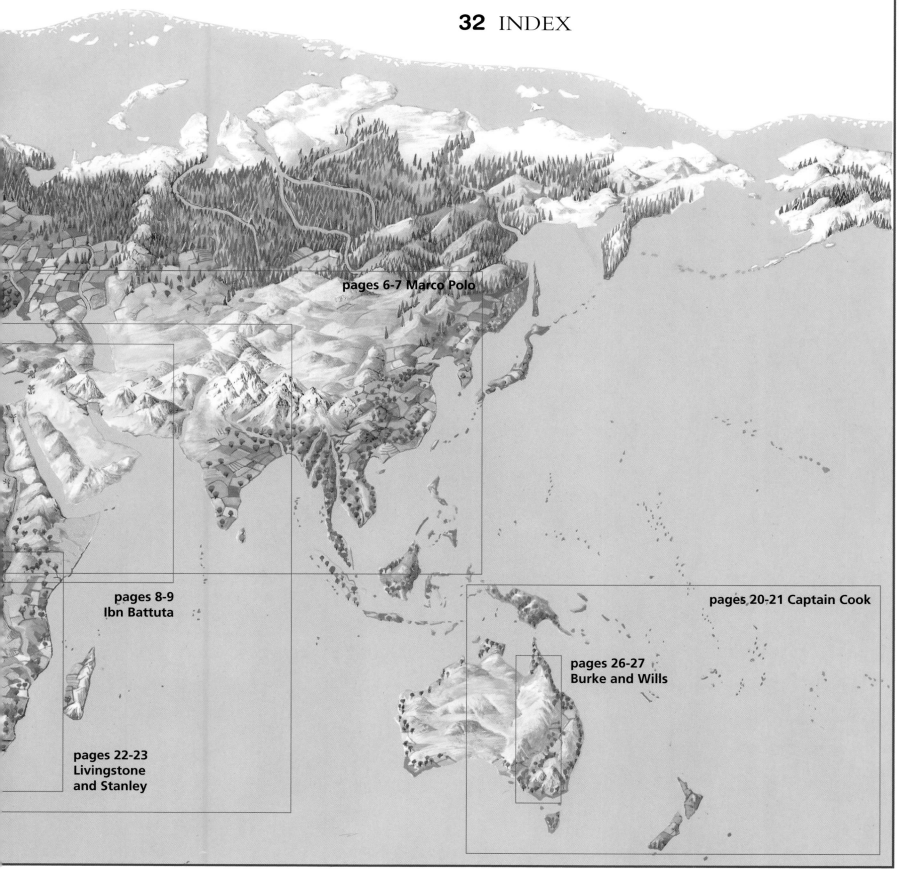

pages 6-7 Marco Polo

pages 8-9 Ibn Battuta

pages 20-21 Captain Cook

pages 26-27 Burke and Wills

pages 22-23 Livingstone and Stanley

THE VIKINGS DISCOVER AMERICA

AROUND 1000 years ago, the Vikings had already settled in Greenland and were exploring the seas to the west. When Erik the Red's son, Leif the Lucky, heard of a sighting of a distant shoreline made by Bjarni Herjolfsson, he was determined to discover that land for himself.

Leif crossed to Baffin Island, before traveling down the coast of Labrador, where he became the first European to set foot on American soil. He spent winter in a place he called Vinland, before returning to Greenland the following spring. His brother Thorvald later repeated Leif's voyage, this time encountering American Indians (known to the Vikings as Skraelings) who attacked him and his men with stones and clubs. The Vikings drove them off, but not before Thorvald was shot with an arrow. A later expedition to colonize Vinland lasted only three years. Far from home and outnumbered by the Skraelings, the Vikings left America forever.

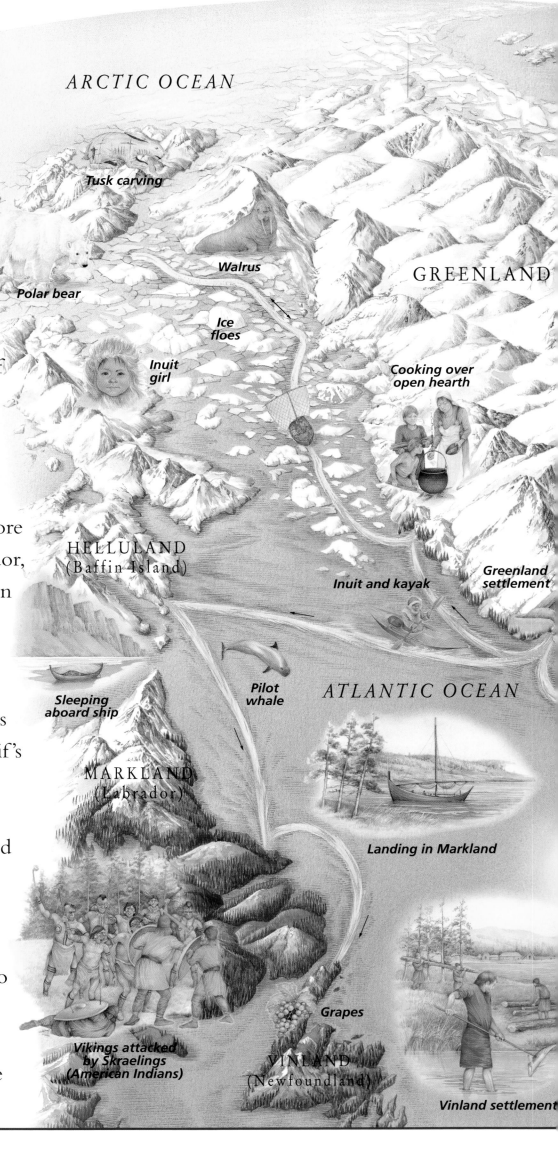

ARCTIC OCEAN

Tusk carving

Walrus

GREENLAND

Polar bear

Ice floes

Inuit girl

Cooking over open hearth

HELLULAND
(Baffin Island)

Inuit and kayak

Greenland settlement

Sleeping aboard ship

Pilot whale

ATLANTIC OCEAN

MARKLAND
(Labrador)

Landing in Markland

Grapes

Vikings attacked by Skraelings (American Indians)

VINLAND
(Newfoundland)

Vinland settlement

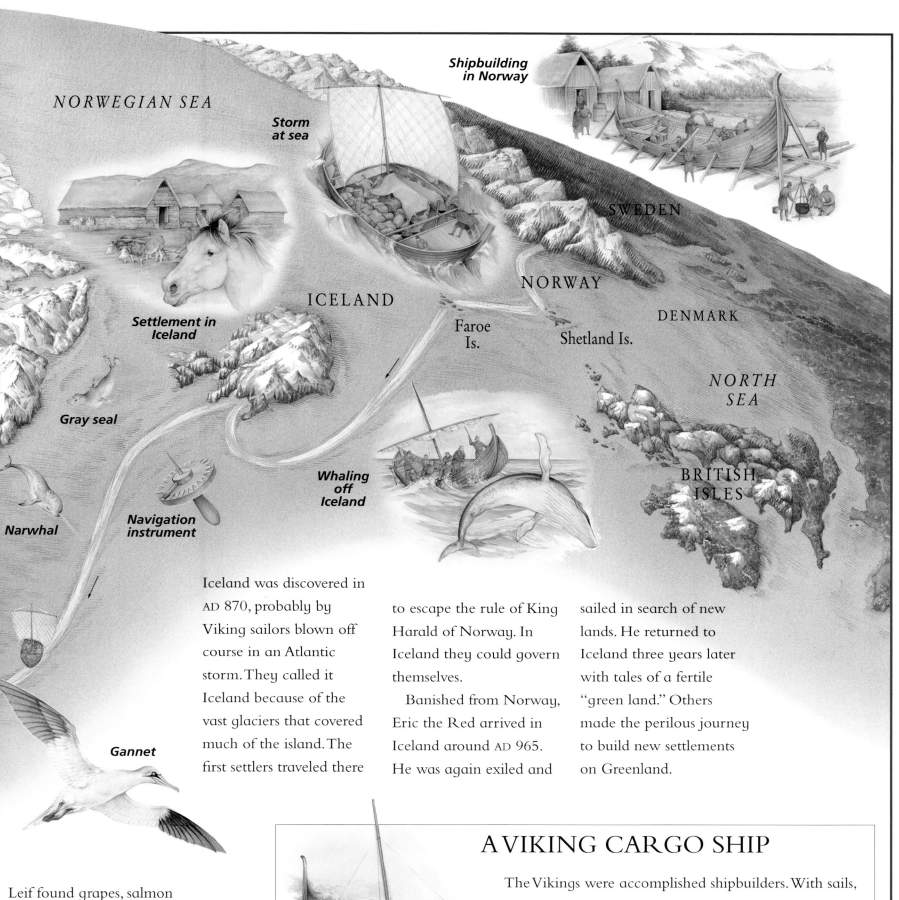

NORWEGIAN SEA

Shipbuilding in Norway

Storm at sea

SWEDEN

ICELAND

Settlement in Iceland

NORWAY

DENMARK

Faroe Is.

Shetland Is.

NORTH SEA

Gray seal

Narwhal

Navigation instrument

Whaling off Iceland

BRITISH ISLES

Gannet

Iceland was discovered in AD 870, probably by Viking sailors blown off course in an Atlantic storm. They called it Iceland because of the vast glaciers that covered much of the island. The first settlers traveled there to escape the rule of King Harald of Norway. In Iceland they could govern themselves.

Banished from Norway, Eric the Red arrived in Iceland around AD 965. He was again exiled and sailed in search of new lands. He returned to Iceland three years later with tales of a fertile "green land." Others made the perilous journey to build new settlements on Greenland.

Leif found grapes, salmon creeks, and pastures in Vinland (it may have been named after "vines," or the old Norse word for meadowland, *vin*). The remains of a Viking settlement were discovered in northern Newfoundland in 1960, leading many to think that this was Vinland.

A VIKING CARGO SHIP

The Vikings were accomplished shipbuilders. With sails, their ships could travel very quickly across windy northern seas. The cargo ships, called *knarrs*, that carried settlers to new lands had wider hulls than those of the narrow longships the Vikings used in warfare. Both kinds of ship were built with overlapping planks. Besides carrying people, a *knarr* had to have room for horses, cattle, and all the stores needed to build a settlement overseas.

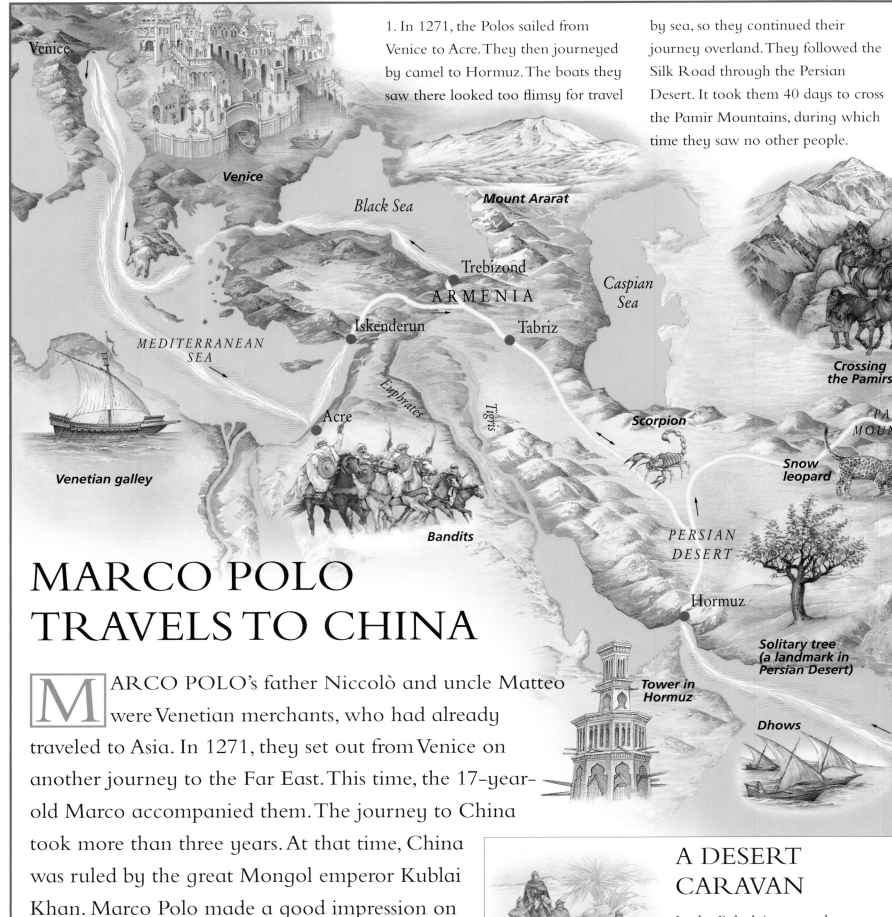

1. In 1271, the Polos sailed from Venice to Acre. They then journeyed by camel to Hormuz. The boats they saw there looked too flimsy for travel by sea, so they continued their journey overland. They followed the Silk Road through the Persian Desert. It took them 40 days to cross the Pamir Mountains, during which time they saw no other people.

Venice

Venice

Black Sea

Mount Ararat

Trebizond

ARMENIA

Caspian Sea

Iskenderun

Tabriz

MEDITERRANEAN SEA

Euphrates

Tigris

Acre

Scorpion

Crossing the Pamirs

PAM MOUN

Snow leopard

Venetian galley

Bandits

PERSIAN DESERT

Hormuz

Solitary tree (a landmark in Persian Desert)

Tower in Hormuz

Dhows

MARCO POLO TRAVELS TO CHINA

MARCO POLO's father Niccolò and uncle Matteo were Venetian merchants, who had already traveled to Asia. In 1271, they set out from Venice on another journey to the Far East. This time, the 17-year-old Marco accompanied them. The journey to China took more than three years. At that time, China was ruled by the great Mongol emperor Kublai Khan. Marco Polo made a good impression on him and became his loyal servant. For the next 17 years, Marco traveled around the empire, reporting back on everything that he saw. In 1292, the Polos left for Venice by sea, escorting a Mongol princess as far as Hormuz.

A DESERT CARAVAN

In the Polos' time, travelers were often attacked by bandits who stole their goods. It was safer to cross the desert in a large group, called a caravan. At night, the travelers camped together for protection.

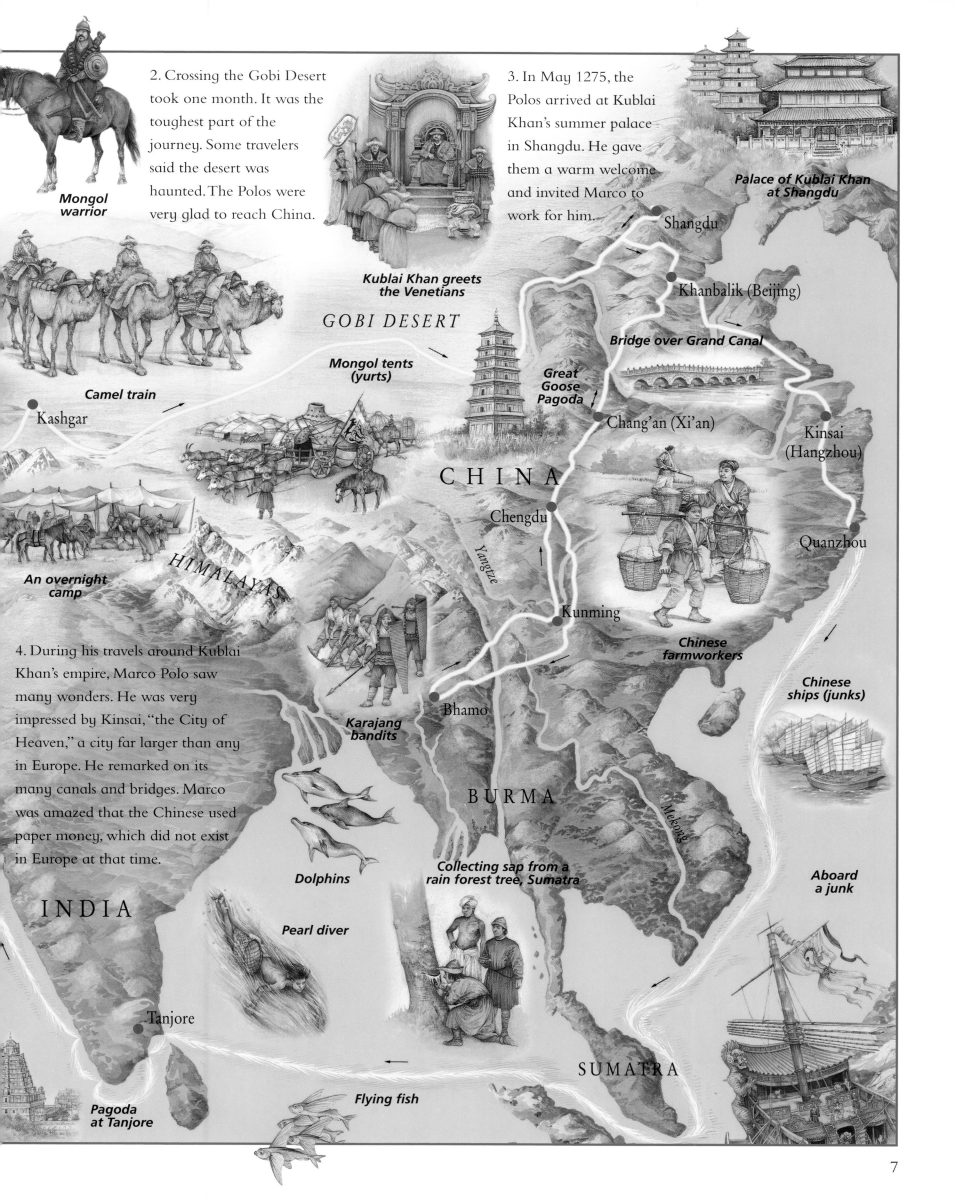

Mongol warrior

2. Crossing the Gobi Desert took one month. It was the toughest part of the journey. Some travelers said the desert was haunted. The Polos were very glad to reach China.

3. In May 1275, the Polos arrived at Kublai Khan's summer palace in Shangdu. He gave them a warm welcome and invited Marco to work for him.

Kublai Khan greets the Venetians

Palace of Kublai Khan at Shangdu

Shangdu

Khanbalik (Beijing)

GOBI DESERT

Mongol tents (yurts)

Great Goose Pagoda

Bridge over Grand Canal

Chang'an (Xi'an)

Camel train

Kashgar

C H I N A

Kinsai (Hangzhou)

Chengdu

Yangtze

Quanzhou

An overnight camp

HIMALAYAS

Kunming

Chinese farmworkers

4. During his travels around Kublai Khan's empire, Marco Polo saw many wonders. He was very impressed by Kinsai, "the City of Heaven," a city far larger than any in Europe. He remarked on its many canals and bridges. Marco was amazed that the Chinese used paper money, which did not exist in Europe at that time.

Karajang bandits

Bhamo

B U R M A

Mekong

Chinese ships (junks)

Dolphins

I N D I A

Pearl diver

Collecting sap from a rain forest tree, Sumatra

Aboard a junk

Tanjore

S U M A T R A

Pagoda at Tanjore

Flying fish

THE TRAVELS OF IBN BATTUTA

D URING THE 14th century, the great Muslim explorer Ibn Battuta traveled more than 70,000 miles throughout Africa, Asia, Arabia, and Europe. His adventures began in 1325 when he set out from Morocco on a *hajj* (pilgrimage) to the Muslim holy city of Mecca in Arabia. This initial journey inspired him to continue traveling around the Islamic world. As a well-educated Muslim, he was welcomed by scholars and rulers wherever he went. Ibn Battuta returned to Morocco in 1349. Just over two years later, he decided to make one last journey across the Sahara Desert to the kingdom of Mali. When he finally returned home, he recorded his amazing journeys in a book known as the *Rihlah*.

Tangier

Algiers

Tunis

MOROCCO

Ibn Battuta

Marrakesh

Getting married

Meeting King of Mali

Attacked by armed robber

Oasis

Niger

SAHARA DESERT

Hoggar mountains

M A L I

Mali

Mosque

Hippos

Camel caravan

1. Ibn Battuta left Tangier in 1325. He joined a camel caravan and headed east. In Alexandria, he saw the Pharos lighthouse, one of the Seven Wonders of the Ancient World. In the holy city of Jerusalem he visited the amazing golden-domed Haram al Sharif mosque. On reaching Mecca, he worshiped at the Muslim shrine called the Kaaba.

Coin

Dome of the rock

MEDITERRANEAN SEA

Tabriz

Tigris

Euphrates

Mosque

Isfahan

Baghdad

Jerusalem

Alexandria

Cairo

Citadel in Cairo

Shiraz

Camel train

Date palms

PERSIAN GULF

Pharos lighthouse

A R A B I A

Nile

Medina

ARABIAN SEA

Mecca

AFRICA

RED SEA

The sacred shrine in Mecca

Zafar

Hajj travelers

Aden

2. From Mecca, Ibn Battuta headed north with another group of pilgrims. They traveled at night by torchlight because it was too hot to travel during the day. In Isfahan and Shiraz, he saw beautiful mosques. He also visited Baghdad where he had an audience with the ruler of the region.

3. In 1327, Ibn Battuta fell ill. He returned to Mecca to rest. When he recovered, he explored the Red Sea and traveled to the port of Aden. Here, he joined a trading ship which sailed south to Mogadishu.

4. Ibn Battuta then traveled down the African coast to Kilwa. Here, he saw Muslim traders exchanging gold for spices. He then sailed to the port of Zafar where he saw horses being shipped to India.

Mogadishu

Dhow

Mombasa

THE SULTAN OF DELHI

Ibn Battuta reached India in 1333. There he was appointed as a judge by the eccentric Sultan of Delhi. In 1342, the Sultan sent Ibn Battuta on a long expedition to meet the Emperor of China.

INDIAN OCEAN

Kilwa

Niña

Santa Maria

Pinta

2. Finding no sign of the rich Asian cities they had expected, the crew sailed on to Cuba, which was inhabited by the friendly Taino people. The Europeans were amazed that they slept in hanging beds called hammocks and smoked tobacco leaves. In November, the crew of the *Pinta* deserted the expedition, disappointed that no treasure had been found.

Christopher Columbus

Christopher Columbus was born in the Italian port of Genoa. Aged 25, he moved to Lisbon in Portugal. He worked on merchant ships that sailed into the Atlantic Ocean and along Africa's west coast. This inspired him to plan his voyage across the Atlantic.

Quadrant

ATLANTIC OCEAN

Landing on San Salvador

Sighting land

NORTH AMERICA

Seabirds

Migrating birds

San Salvador

BAHAMAS IS.

Indian dugout canoes

Pineapple

Taino village

CUBA

HISPANIOLA

JAMAICA

CENTRAL AMERICA

Native smoking tobacco

Wreck of Santa Maria

COLUMBUS SAILS ACROSS THE ATLANTIC

Lisbon SPAIN

Palos

Leaving Palos

Loading supplies

AFRICA

Canary Is.

Life on board

Hourglass

Sailing through the floating weed of the Sargasso Sea

1. The fleet sailed from Palos in 1492. To reassure his restless crew during the voyage, Columbus kept a false log, which indicated that they were not as far from Spain as they really were. After several false alarms, land was sighted in October. The crew landed on a tiny island which they named San Salvador ("Holy Saviour"). Here they met friendly natives. Thinking he had arrived in the East Indies, Columbus called them "Indians." This name has been used ever since.

In December, the *anta María* was recked off Hispaniola, hich Columbus had aimed for Spain. He dered his men to uild a fort on the land and left 39 of em behind when he eaded back to Spain.

ilding a fort

Royal reception on return to Spain

BY THE LATE 15th century, most educated people agreed that the Earth was round. While others attempted to reach Asia by sailing around Africa *(see pages 12-13)*, the Genoese sailor Christopher Columbus believed that China and Japan could just as easily be reached by sailing west across the Atlantic. But, with the Vikings' discoveries long forgotten, he had no idea that the Americas existed. He initially asked King John II of Portugal to sponsor his expedition. However, the king thought that Columbus had miscalculated the size of the Atlantic, so he refused to give him money. Columbus then turned to King Ferdinand and Queen Isabella of Spain. They were impressed by his plan and agreed to finance his voyage. In 1492, he set sail from Spain with three ships under his command: the flagship *Santa María* and the smaller caravels, the *Niña* and the *Pinta*. When he arrived in the Caribbean, Columbus was disappointed not to come across the busy Chinese ports he had expected. In fact, he had accidentally landed in the Americas.

VASCO DA GAMA SAILS TO INDIA

Vasco da Gama

IN THE LATE 15th century, Europeans were keen to find a new sea route to the Far East. They wanted to trade independently with China, Japan, and India without having to rely on the Silk Road *(see page 6)*, a trade route which led overland through central Asia and which was at that time under the control of Muslims.

In July 1497, under the orders of King Manuel I, Portuguese explorer Vasco da Gama set sail from Lisbon in the hope of finding a new route to India. He set out with four ships under his command: two large merchant ships, the *São Gabriel* and the *São Rafael*, the *Berrio*, a light caravel, and an unnamed store ship (which was later damaged in a storm and abandoned). The fleet followed a southwesterly route before swinging east round the Cape of Good Hope. They then sailed up the east coast of Africa. On their way, they set up stone columns, called *padrãos*. These would act as signposts for future sailors. With the assistance of an Arab navigator, they crossed the Indian Ocean in just 23 days, arriving at Calicut in southern India.

SPAIN

PORTUGAL
Lisbon

The fleet sets sail

Canary
Is.

Gull

Cape Verde
Is.

*Green
turtle*

ATLANTIC
OCEAN

Dolphin

*Using an astrolabe
for navigation*

SOUTH
AMERICA

Da Gama's fleet

*Suffering
from scurvy*

*Sperm
whale*

1. To avoid unfavorable winds and currents, da Gama boldly led his fleet out into the Atlantic instead of along the west coast of Africa. They did not see land for three months. The crew feared that they would sail off the edge of the earth.

MEDITERRANEAN SEA

2. The Portuguese had hoped to trade with the rulers of East Africa. However, the Sultan of Mozambique was insulted by the cheap trinkets that they offered him. They received a warmer welcome in Malindi, where the Sultan exchanged food and spices for Portuguese goods.

3. The Hindu ruler of Calicut, the Zamorin, welcomed da Gama. However, he refused to trade with the Portuguese. Their goods, including beads, cloth, and olive oil, were of no interest to the rich ruler. Da Gama and his men left India with only a modest cargo of spices.

The Zamorin greets da Gama

ARABIA

INDIA

Dhow

Calicut

Frigatebird

Padrão

Malindi

INDIAN OCEAN

Flying fish

Mombasa

Arrival at Malindi

AFRICA

Mozambique

Sultan of Mozambique

Burning the store ship

St. Helena Bay

Hottentots

Cape of Good Hope

Mossel Bay

ARRIVAL IN INDIA

When Vasco da Gama and his men finally reached Calicut, boats swarmed around the ships, offering them fresh fruit and vegetables for sale. The Portuguese sailors thought they had arrived in a land of riches. But they were unable to sell their goods to the Indian ruler, so they traded what they could for spices in the markets of Calicut.

1. In 1519, Magellan's fleet sailed down the coast of South America, searching for a passage through to another ocean. They spent the winter months in San Julián. Here, the crew saw local natives whom they called *patagones*, or "big feet." Three of the ships mutinied, but Magellan executed three of the ring-leaders and stranded two more ashore. Later, two of the ships disappeared. They later returned having found the passage that was to be called the Strait of Magellan. In October 1520, the fleet sailed through this hazardous channel into the Pacific Ocean.

THE *TRINIDAD*

Magellan set out with five ships and about 260 men. His flagship was the *Trinidad,* the only ship in the fleet armed with cannon, as defense against pirates. The wooden ship, only about 100 feet long, had to carry sufficient food for a long journey. Valuable supplies were lost when one of the other ships, the *Santiago*, was wrecked off the coast of South America. Soon afterwards,

the crew of the *San Antonio* mutinied and abandoned the expedition. The *Trinidad*, along with her cargo of spices bound for Spain, was captured by Portuguese sailors in the Spice Islands. The *Victoria* was the only ship to return to Spain in 1522, weathering fierce storms and the threat of Portuguese attack. Of Magellan's original crew there were just 18 survivors on board, plus four Spice Islanders.

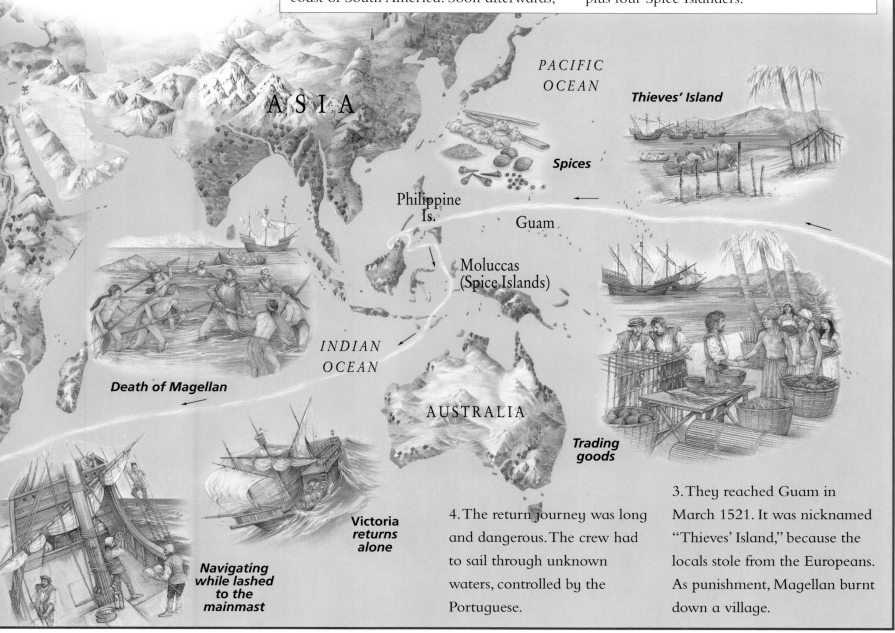

PACIFIC OCEAN

ASIA

Thieves' Island

Spices

Philippine Is.

Guam

Moluccas (Spice Islands)

INDIAN OCEAN

Death of Magellan

AUSTRALIA

Trading goods

Victoria returns alone

Navigating while lashed to the mainmast

4. The return journey was long and dangerous. The crew had to sail through unknown waters, controlled by the Portuguese.

3. They reached Guam in March 1521. It was nicknamed "Thieves' Island," because the locals stole from the Europeans. As punishment, Magellan burnt down a village.

PIZARRO CONQUERS THE INCA EMPIRE

A SMALL BAND of Spanish soldiers under the command of Francisco Pizarro arrived in Inca lands in 1532. Known as *conquistadores*, they were in search of an unknown kingdom rumored to be rich with gold. They found an empire riven by civil war. Leading a force of just 177 men, Pizarro crossed the Andes to meet the Inca Emperor, Atahuallpa, and his vast army in Cajamarca. Despite receiving a ransom of more than 20 tons of gold and silver, the Spaniards murdered Atahuallpa and marched on to the Inca capital city, Cuzco. Although many Inca warriors kept up resistance for 40 years, the Inca Empire fell under Spanish rule.

Despite his soldiers being outnumbered, Pizarro devised a plan to defeat the Inca army. Atahuallpa and around 3000 of his followers arrived in the square at Cajamarca unarmed. On hearing a signal from their leader, Pizarro's horsemen charged from their hiding places around the square and slaughtered thousands of Indians. Atahuallpa was captured by Pizarro himself.

Atahuallpa

Quito

Worshipping the Sun God

Tomebamba (Cuenca)

Terrace farming

Rope bridge

Huancabamba

Atahuallpa arrives in Cajamarca

Tumbes

Paved road

Harvesting corn

Gold figurine

Cajamarca

Galleons

Raft

Piura

A N D

PERUVIAN DES

Chasquis (message runner)

Sacsahuaman, an Inca fortress, lay on a hill to the west of Cuzco. It was enclosed by immense, zigzagging walls more than 50 feet high. About 10,000 people could have found refuge inside it. It did not save Cuzco from capture by the Spanish, however.

View over Cuzco

Crossing a creek

Llama

Lake Titicaca

Machu Picchu

Cuzco

Apurimac

Condor

Inca warriors attack Spaniards

Huamanga (Ayacucho)

Reed boat on Lake Titicaca

Bridge across the Apurimac

M O U N T A I N S

Huanuco

Stepped road

Jauja

Inspector of bridges

Inca warrior

Alpaca carrying firewood

Pizarro

PACIFIC OCEAN

Cuzco, built high in the mountains, was the Inca capital. Cuzco means "navel of the world" in Quechua, the language of the Incas. The walls of the thatch-roofed buildings were made out of stone. The irregularly-shaped blocks were precisely fitted together by Inca workers with great skill. Cuzco's palaces, temples, and warehouses bulged with treasures and goods.

Following the execution of Atahuallpa in August 1533, Pizarro set off for Cuzco. The Spaniards fought off attacks by Inca warriors at Jauja and elsewhere. Many died trying to defend Cuzco, which Pizarro captured in November.

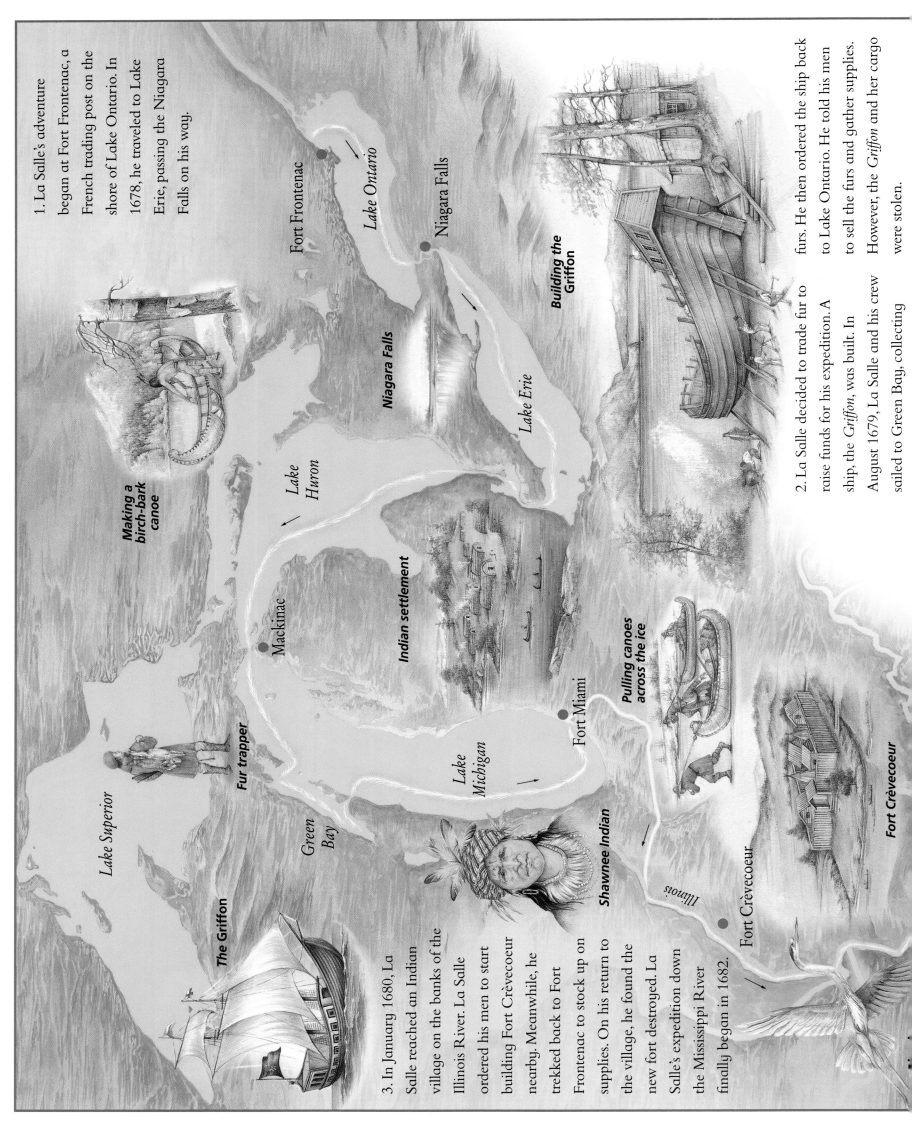

1. La Salle's adventure began at Fort Frontenac, a French trading post on the shore of Lake Ontario. In 1678, he traveled to Lake Erie, passing the Niagara Falls on his way.

Fort Frontenac

Lake Ontario

Niagara Falls

Building the Griffon

2. La Salle decided to trade fur to raise funds for his expedition. A ship, the *Griffon*, was built. In August 1679, La Salle and his crew sailed to Green Bay, collecting furs. He then ordered the ship back to Lake Ontario. He told his men to sell the furs and gather supplies. However, the *Griffon* and her cargo were stolen.

Niagara Falls

Lake Erie

Making a birch-bark canoe

Lake Huron

Indian settlement

Mackinac

Fur trapper

Lake Superior

Green Bay

The Griffon

Fort Miami

Pulling canoes across the ice

Lake Michigan

Shawnee Indian

Illinois

Fort Crèvecoeur

Fort Crèvecoeur

3. In January 1680, La Salle reached an Indian village on the banks of the Illinois River. La Salle ordered his men to start building Fort Crèvecoeur nearby. Meanwhile, he trekked back to Fort Frontenac to stock up on supplies. On his return to the village, he found the new fort destroyed. La Salle's expedition down the Mississippi River finally began in 1682.

LA SALLE TRAVELS DOWN THE MISSISSIPPI RIVER

B Y THE 1600s, a chain of French and English colonies had been established along the east coast of North America. However, the vast American interior remained largely unexplored. French explorer Réné Robert de la Salle was keen to expand the territory occupied by France. He formed a plan to build a chain of French forts along the Mississippi River, the upper reaches of which had been already explored in 1673. Although the French king, Louis XIV, approved of La Salle's proposal, he refused to provide any money. La Salle had to raise his funds for the expedition by trading furs. He finally began his voyage down the "father of waters" in February 1682. By April, he had reached the mouth of the Mississippi and proudly claimed all of the land around it for France. He named it Louisiana in honor of the king.

La Salle had trained as a priest before deciding to pursue a life of adventure in America. He discovered a lot about the customs of the Indians he met on his travels. La Salle made a second voyage by sea to the mouth of the Mississippi in 1687. However, the expedition was not a success. La Salle was killed when his own men turned on him.

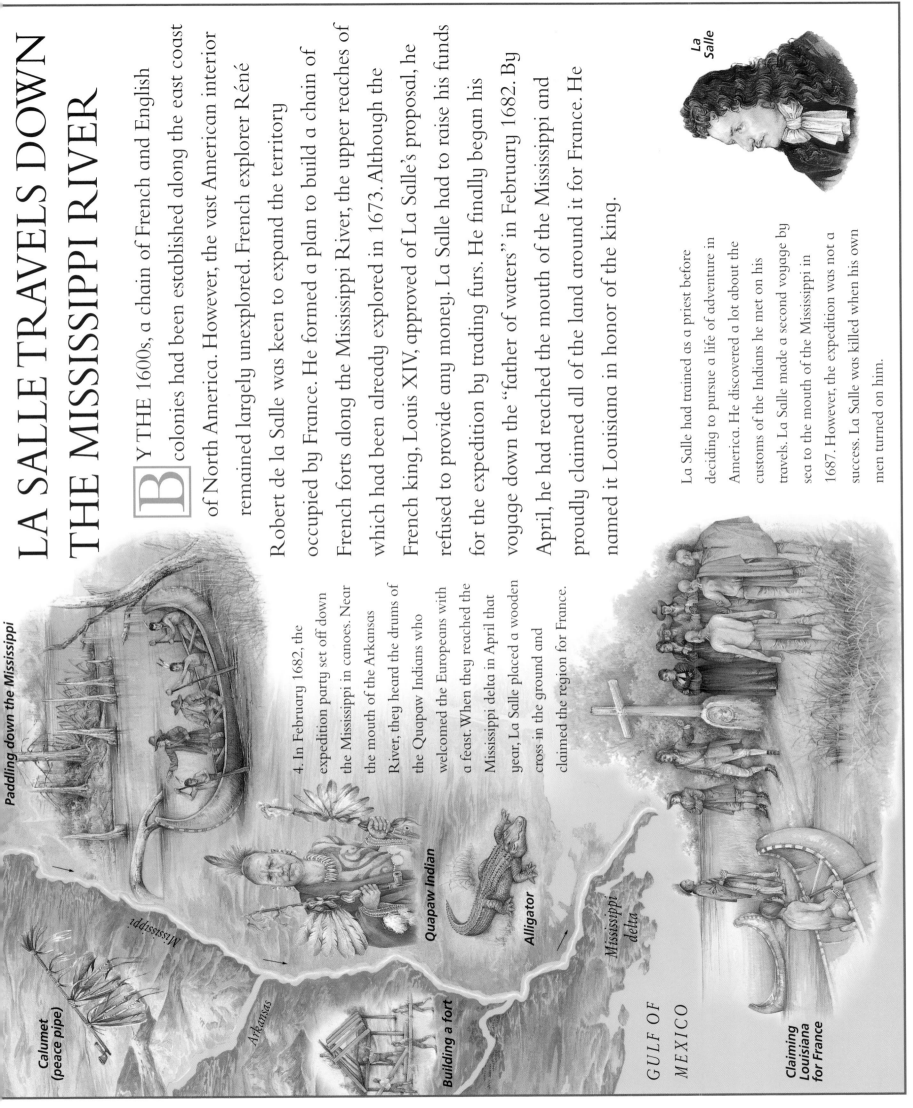

La Salle

Paddling down the Mississippi

4. In February 1682, the expedition party set off down the Mississippi in canoes. Near the mouth of the Arkansas River, they heard the drums of the Quapaw Indians who welcomed the Europeans with a feast. When they reached the Mississippi delta in April that year, La Salle placed a wooden cross in the ground and claimed the region for France.

Calumet (peace pipe)

Mississippi

Arkansas

Quapaw Indian

Alligator

Building a fort

Mississippi delta

GULF OF MEXICO

Claiming Louisiana for France

Bird of paradise

Stingray

NEW GUINEA

Dugong

4. In August 1770, Cook claimed Eastern Australia for Britain, naming it New South Wales. The *Endeavour* then headed home via the Cape of Good Hope. They arrived in England in July 1771. Not one member of the crew had died of scurvy, a disease that had previously killed many sailors. Cook had realized that eating citrus fruit helped prevent the illness.

GREAT BARRIER REEF

Claiming New South Wales

3. Cook sailed slowly up Australia's east coast. In June 1770, the *Endeavour* ran aground on the Great Barrier Reef. It took several weeks to repair the vessel. Cook then continued north.

Hunting kangaroos

AUSTRALIA

Red honeysuckle

Collecting samples

Aground on Great Barrier Reef

Hostile Maori warboats

Botany Bay

North Island

Captain James Cook

TASMANIA

Maori family

NEW ZEALAND

2. In April 1770, Cook headed west to Australia. His ship anchored at Stingray Bay, later renamed Botany Bay as Joseph Banks had found so many new plant species there. The explorers were amazed by the unusual local wildlife, including kangaroos, which they thought were "some kind of stag."

South Island

James Cook worked on merchant ships for nine years before joining the Royal Navy in 1755. As he was already an experienced seaman and an excellent navigator, he was rapidly promoted.

Maori

1. The *Endeavour* left England in August 1768. Cook was in command of a crew of 80 men and 11 scientists, including Joseph Banks. In April 1769, they reached Tahiti. They built a small fort and observed the transit of Venus on June 3rd. Cook then announced the second part of the mission. The party reluctantly left the beautiful island in August and headed south. Finding no sign of Terra Australis, Cook then sailed to New Zealand, where he was met by hostile Maori natives. He sailed around both the North and South Islands, mapping the coast.

THE *ENDEAVOUR*

Captain Cook chose an unusual vessel for his voyage. The *Endeavour* was a converted collier, or coal ship, similar to those he had worked on as a young man. It was a sturdy and slow-moving vessel that could carry a large crew. It also had storage space for scientific equipment—and fresh food for the crew, including meat, vegetables, and fruit juices.

Tahiti

Observing the transit of Venus

Tahiti

Aboard the Endeavour

Dolphins

Red-tailed tropic bird

SOUTH PACIFIC OCEAN

HMS Endeavour

CAPTAIN COOK SAILS THE SOUTH SEAS

IN 1768, the British Royal Society chose James Cook to captain a scientific expedition to Tahiti, in the South Pacific Ocean. Astronomers had predicted that Venus would pass in front of the Sun in June 1769. By observing this from different points around the globe, they hoped to measure the distance of the Sun from Earth accurately. Cook was also given an additional set of sealed instructions, which he was to read on arrival in Tahiti. These told him to locate *Terra Australis Incognita*, or "Unknown Southern Land," and to claim it for Great Britain. But Cook never found this great southern continent.

3. In 1874, Stanley arrived in Zanzibar with a huge expedition party and trekked to Lake Victoria. He explored the lake in the Lady Alice, a boat designed to be broken into pieces that were easily carried. He proved that Lake Victoria was the source of the Nile.

4. Stanley then led his team overland to Ujiji. They explored Lake Tanganyika, before canoeing down the Lualaba River into the last great unknown river in Africa, the Congo. They struggled through rapids, waterfalls, and dense jungle before reaching Boma in August 1877. Fewer than half of Stanley's men survived.

2. In 1853, Livingstone canoed up the Zambezi with 27 men from the Kololo tribe. They continued westwards towards the coast, reaching Luanda in May 1854. After resting for several months, they returned to Sesheke. They then traveled down the Zambezi, arriving at Quelimane in 1856.

Henry Morton Stanley

The expedition sets off

Zanzibar

Mikindani

Ruvuma

Native settlement

Dugout canoe

Quelimane

Shire

Ma Robert steamboat

Sena

Lake Victoria

Lady Alice

Canoe on Lake Tanganyika

Lake Nyasa

Giraffe

Elephant

Zambezi

Medicine chest

Ujiji

Lake Bangweulu

Lady Alice in pieces

Attack by cannibals

Nyangwe

Lake Tanganyika

Carrying Livingstone's body

Canoeing up the Zambezi

Slaves

Lualaba

Traveling down Congo River

Congo

Victoria Falls

Chimpanzees

Zambezi

Victoria Falls

Sesheke

Traveling to Lake Ngami

Kasai

Luanda

Lake Ngami

Boma

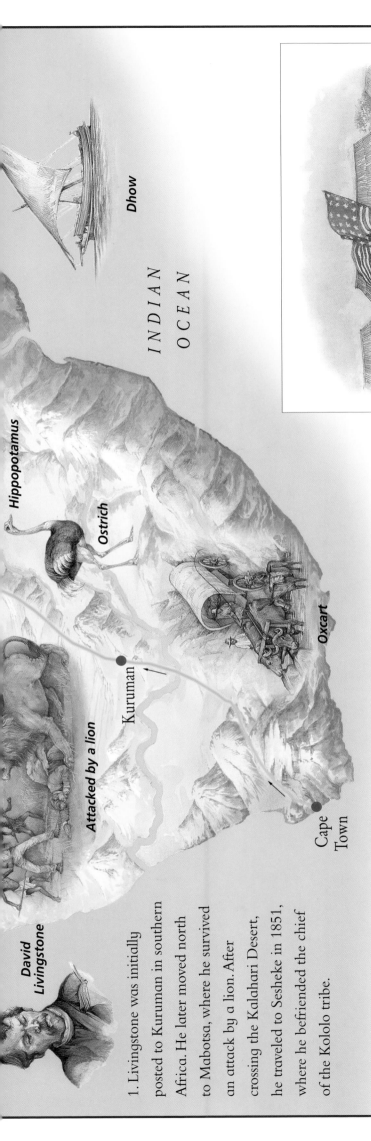

David Livingstone

Hippopotamus

Attacked by a lion

Ostrich

Oxcart

Kuruman

Cape Town

Dhow

I N D I A N
O C E A N

1. Livingstone was initially posted to Kuruman in southern Africa. He later moved north to Mabotsa, where he survived an attack by a lion. After crossing the Kalahari Desert, he traveled to Sesheke in 1851, where he befriended the chief of the Kololo tribe.

ACROSS AFRICA WITH LIVINGSTONE AND STANLEY

COTSMAN David Livingstone moved to Africa in 1841, hoping to convert the native peoples to Christianity. In 1849, he made the first of a series of journeys, trekking across the Kalahari Desert by ox-cart to Lake Ngami. He decided to explore the river system to the north of the lake, hoping to find a route into central Africa for British missionaries and traders. He traveled the length of the Zambezi River and became the first white man to see the Victoria Falls, known to the natives as "the smoke that thunders." On later journeys, Livingstone explored the Zambezi and Shire rivers and Lake Nyasa by steamboat. Determined to find the source of the River Nile, he eventually died, sick and weak, near the shores of Lake Bangweulu in May 1873. His African companions carried his body more than 600 miles to the coast.

MEETING AT UJIJI

In 1871, American journalist Henry Stanley went in search of Livingstone, who had disappeared several years previously. Eight months after setting out from Zanzibar, Stanley found him at Ujiji, a town on the shore of Lake Tanganyika. He greeted him with the now-famous words "Dr Livingstone, I presume?" Together the two men explored the lake, discovering that it was not, in fact, the source of the Nile. Stanley left in March 1872, but Livingstone refused to return to England with him.

Willamette Valley, Oregon was the chosen destination of many of the travelers. It was reached after a very difficult climb over the mountains, impassable in winter. Some risked rafting down the treacherous Columbia River for the last few hundred miles.

Rafting down the river

The Rocky Mountains were the first major obstacle the travelers had to face. Fur trappers, called mountain men, who knew the Rockies well from hunting beaver, had already discovered a way across the Platte River. They guided the travellers through South Pass, a 20-mile low saddle across the mountains.

PACIFIC OCEAN

Portland

Columbia

The Dalles

OREGON TRAIL

Mission station, Oregon

Grizzly bear

O R E G O N

Fort Boise

Snake

Friendly encounters with Indians

Fort Hall

Mountain man

CALIFORNIA TRAIL

Ox skull

Cooking over buffalo chips

C A L I F O R N I A

Arriving in Oregon

Humboldt

Great Salt Lake

Fort Bridge

Soaking wagon wheels

Salt Lake City

Sutter's Fort (Sacramento)

Sidewinder

San Francisco

Mormons on Trail

San Francisco

Panning for gold

The California Trail led the travelers across dusty deserts and high mountains to the fertile Sacramento Valley. On the way, many of their animals perished in the searing heat. Wagon wheels were soaked to prevent the iron rims falling off the dried-out, shrunken wheels.

The Mormons, a group within the Christian Church, were driven out of Illinois in 1846. They went in search of a new home, following the Trail part of the way before striking out for the Great Salt Lake.

The lands crossed by the Oregon Trail were home to many Indian tribes. They had lived there for thousands of years, hunting buffalo, trapping, and fishing. They lived in villages of tepees, tents made from sticks and buffalo hides. Different tribes frequently fought one another over hunting territory.

Indians hunting buffalo

FOLLOWING THE OREGON TRAIL

BY THE 1840s, the the lands to the west of the Mississippi River had become part of the United States. People heard that Oregon, on the Pacific coast, was lush and green. With so little farming land available in the east, many decided to leave their homes for ever and make the 1800-mile journey west. Over the next 25 years, nearly half a million people trudged along what came to be known as the Oregon and California Trails. But it was a hard and dangerous trip across the "Great American Desert." Many fell victim to disease, and almost all suffered from hunger, thirst, and exhaustion.

Independence Rock

h Pass

Fort Laramie

Fort Laramie

North Platte

Corral

River crossing

Missouri riverboat

Ferry across the river

Chimney Rock

Platte

Fort Kearny

Missouri

Sioux Indian

Independence

Kansas

ON THE WAGON TRAIN

Settlers bound for Oregon traveled in small farm wagons with the drivers walking alongside. Only young children and the sick rode in the wagon. Water was stored in a barrel strapped to the outside. Steep descents were often a problem: The travelers tied tree trunks to the rear wheels to act as brakes.

At the start of the Trail, hundreds camped outside Independence, Missouri. Settlers usually traveled together in large groups.

Camping

BURKE AND WILLS CROSS AUSTRALIA

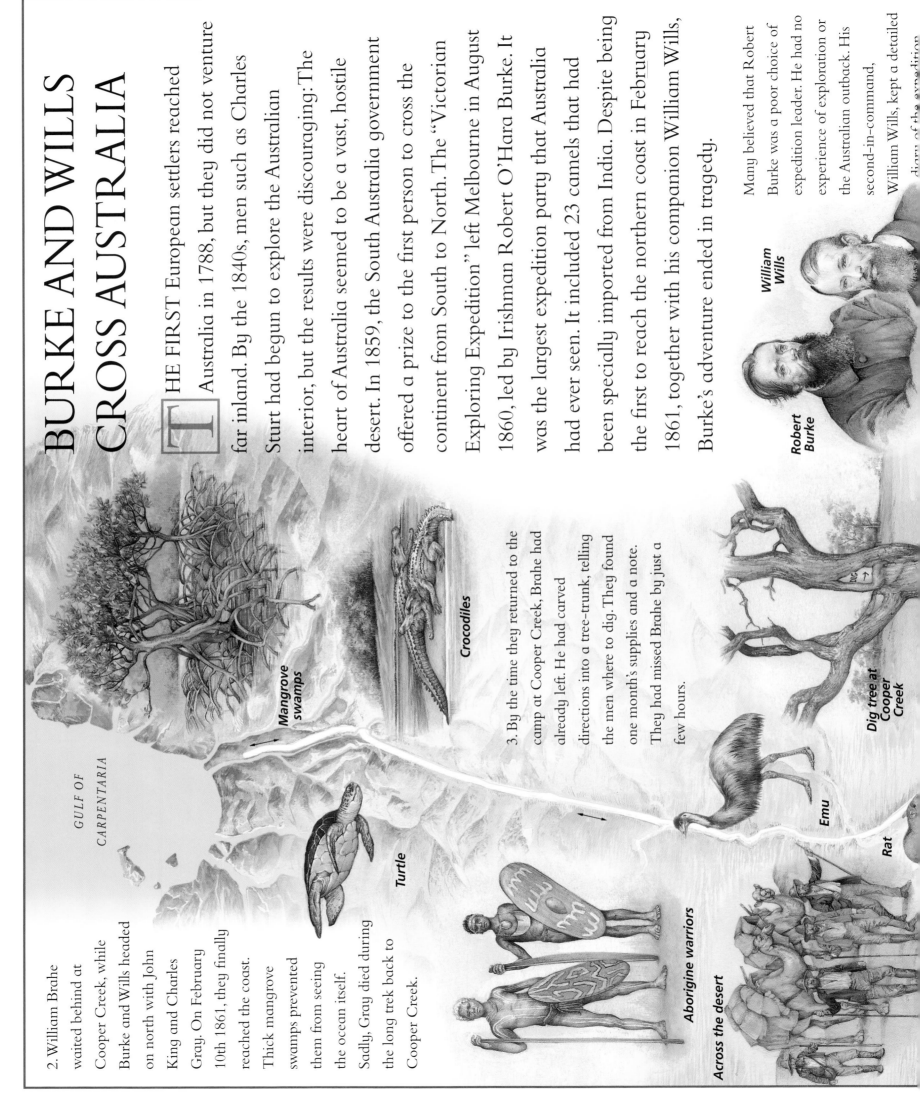

THE FIRST European settlers reached Australia in 1788, but they did not venture far inland. By the 1840s, men such as Charles Sturt had begun to explore the Australian interior, but the results were discouraging: The heart of Australia seemed to be a vast, hostile desert. In 1859, the South Australia government offered a prize to the first person to cross the continent from South to North. The "Victorian Exploring Expedition" left Melbourne in August 1860, led by Irishman Robert O'Hara Burke. It was the largest expedition party that Australia had ever seen. It included 23 camels that had been specially imported from India. Despite being the first to reach the northern coast in February 1861, together with his companion William Wills, Burke's adventure ended in tragedy.

2. William Brahe waited behind at Cooper Creek, while Burke and Wills headed on north with John King and Charles Gray. On February 10th 1861, they finally reached the coast. Thick mangrove swamps prevented them from seeing the ocean itself. Sadly, Gray died during the long trek back to Cooper Creek.

3. By the time they returned to the camp at Cooper Creek, Brahe had already left. He had carved directions into a tree-trunk, telling the men where to dig. They found one month's supplies and a note. They had missed Brahe by just a few hours.

Many believed that Robert Burke was a poor choice of expedition leader. He had no experience of exploration or the Australian outback. His second-in-command, William Wills, kept a detailed diary of the expedition

GULF OF CARPENTARIA

Mangrove swamps

Crocodiles

Turtle

Emu

Rat

Aborigine warriors

Across the desert

Dig tree at Cooper Creek

William Wills

Robert Burke

Aboriginal rock art

1. In October 1860, the expedition party reached Mootwingee, an area which the aborigines believed to be sacred. Despite the summer heat, Burke decided to press on with a few companions to Cooper Creek, where water and food were plentiful.

Struggling to Mount Hopeless

4. Instead of chasing after Brahe, Burke decided that they should head for Mount Hopeless, a police post 150 miles from Cooper Creek. When their supplies ran out, they ate a bush plant called nardoo. But, weakened by hunger, Burke and Wills did not have the strength to survive. They died in June 1861. King was kept alive by friendly aborigines who gave him cooked rats to eat. He was found by a rescue party several months later.

Cooper

Dingo

MOOTWINGEE

Nardoo and pods

Snake

Menindee

Didgeridoo

Murray

Kangaroo

Baldranald

Swan Hill

Platypus

Bendigo

Melbourne

Kangaroo rat

The expedition crosses the Australian outback

Setting off from Melbourne

27

ATLANTIC OCEAN

Skua

Blue whale

Playing soccer on the ice

Leopard seal

WEDDELL SEA

The *Endurance* trapped in the ice

Iceberg

Emperor penguins

The *Endurance* trapped in the ice

Dog igloos

1. The *Endurance* was only about 100 miles from the coastline of the Antarctic continent when, on January 18th 1915, ice floes packed around the ship. She was stuck fast—"frozen like an almond in a toffee," as one crew member wrote. The crew tried to free her, but to no avail.

SHACKLETON'S AMAZING ESCAPE

A BRITISH expedition to cross Antarctica from coast to coast set sail on the *Endurance* from South Georgia, on December 5th 1914. The crew of 27 men was led by Sir Ernest Shackleton, an experienced polar explorer.

The *Endurance* was to sail across the iceberg-filled Weddell Sea to Antarctica, but she never made her destination. The sea froze and the ship became trapped in the pack ice. After drifting northwards, she eventually broke up. Shackleton and his crew had to camp out on the ice before they were able to launch their lifeboats.

The boats crossed to Elephant Island. Leaving behind most of his crew, Shackleton and five companions set out for South Georgia to seek help. They landed on the wrong side of the island, and so they were forced to cross the mountains on foot to reach the manned whaling station on the opposite side. Nearly five months later the rest of the crew on Elephant Island were picked up. Not a single life was lost on the expedition.

Two expeditions set out to reach the South Pole in 1911. Robert Scott led the British, Roald Amundsen the Norwegians. Scott's men were held up by blizzards. Amundsen's team reached the Pole 33 days ahead of Scott in December 1911.

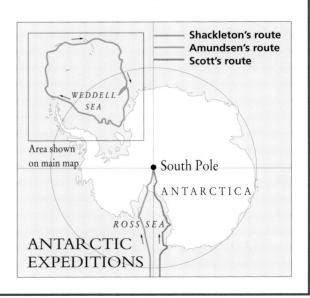

Shackleton's route
Amundsen's route
Scott's route

WEDDELL SEA

Area shown on main map

South Pole

ANTARCTICA

ROSS SEA

ANTARCTIC EXPEDITIONS

THE KON-TIKI EXPEDITION

FOR YEARS, experts believed that the inhabitants of the Polynesian Islands had originally come from Asia. But Norwegian Thor Heyerdahl noticed that some ancient statues on a Polynesian island were very similar to some he had seen in Bolivia. Heyerdahl began to think that the Polynesians had actually originated in South America, not Asia. In order to test his theory, he had to prove that people could have sailed from Peru to the Pacific Islands on their simple wooden rafts. So, he and five other men set sail in such a raft, the *Kon-Tiki,* in 1947. The voyage was a great success, but scientists now believe the Polynesians originated in Southeast Asia.

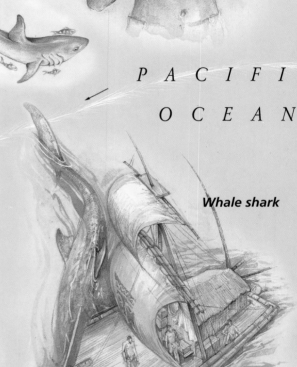

Snakefish aboard!

Shark with pilot fish

P A C I F I C
O C E A N

Whale shark

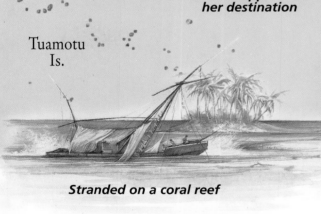

Raroia

Kon-Tiki *approaches her destination*

Tuamotu Is.

Stranded on a coral reef

Man overboard

THE CREW

The crew of the *Kon-Tiki* consisted of five Norwegians and one Swede. Although none was an experienced sailor, they soon got used to life at sea. They learned to catch small sharks by hand, which they then cooked and ate. One day, a huge whale shark—a peaceful giant, harmless to humans—swam underneath *Kon-Tiki*. It could easily have capsized the raft. Luckily, no one was injured.

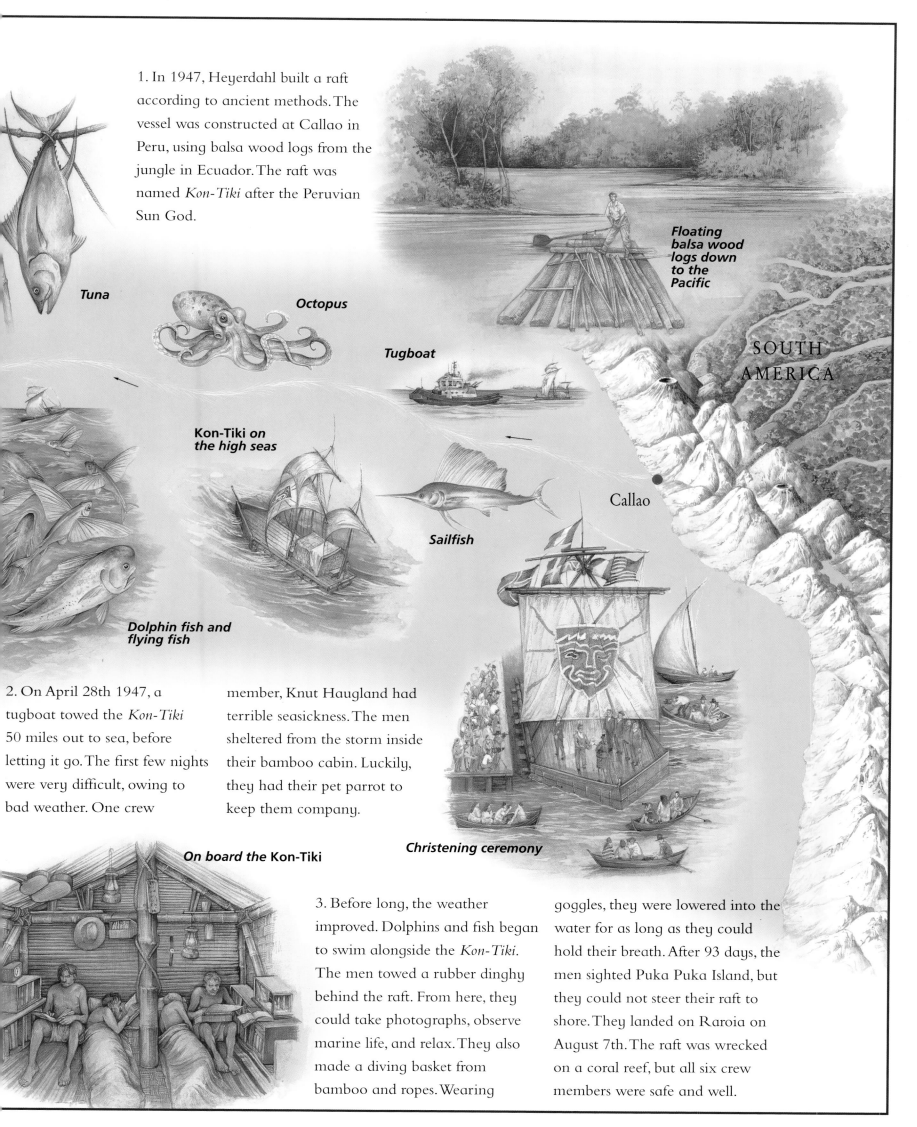

1. In 1947, Heyerdahl built a raft according to ancient methods. The vessel was constructed at Callao in Peru, using balsa wood logs from the jungle in Ecuador. The raft was named *Kon-Tiki* after the Peruvian Sun God.

Floating balsa wood logs down to the Pacific

Tuna

Octopus

Tugboat

SOUTH AMERICA

Kon-Tiki on the high seas

Sailfish

Callao

Dolphin fish and flying fish

2. On April 28th 1947, a tugboat towed the *Kon-Tiki* 50 miles out to sea, before letting it go. The first few nights were very difficult, owing to bad weather. One crew member, Knut Haugland had terrible seasickness. The men sheltered from the storm inside their bamboo cabin. Luckily, they had their pet parrot to keep them company.

Christening ceremony

On board the Kon-Tiki

3. Before long, the weather improved. Dolphins and fish began to swim alongside the *Kon-Tiki*. The men towed a rubber dinghy behind the raft. From here, they could take photographs, observe marine life, and relax. They also made a diving basket from bamboo and ropes. Wearing goggles, they were lowered into the water for as long as they could hold their breath. After 93 days, the men sighted Puka Puka Island, but they could not steer their raft to shore. They landed on Raroia on August 7th. The raft was wrecked on a coral reef, but all six crew members were safe and well.

INDEX

Published in the United States, Canada, and Puerto Rico by Hammond World Atlas Corporation, Springfield, New Jersey 07081   www.hammondmap.com

Copyright © 2006 Orpheus Books Ltd

Created and produced by Rachel Coombs, Nicholas Harris, Sarah Harrison, Sarah Hartley and Emma Helbrough, Orpheus Books Ltd

Illustrators Gary Hincks, Nicki Palin

ISBN 0-8437-0919-7

Printed and bound in China.